CAREERS MAKING A DIFFERENCE

HELPING THOSE WITH DISABILITIES

CAREERS MAKING A DIFFERENCE

HELPING ANIMALS

HELPING CHILDREN

HELPING SENIORS

HELPING THOSE IN POVERTY

HELPING THOSE WITH ADDICTIONS

HELPING THOSE WITH DISABILITIES

HELPING THOSE WITH MENTAL ILLNESSES

HELPING TO PROTECT THE ENVIRONMENT

HELPING VICTIMS

CAREERS MAKING A DIFFERENCE

HELPING THOSE
WITH DISABILITIES

AMANDA TURNER

MASON CREST

PHILADELPHIA
MIAMI

MASON CREST

450 Parkway Drive, Suite D, Broomall, Pennsylvania 19008
(866) MCP-BOOK (toll-free) • www.masoncrest.com

Printed in the United States of America

First printing
9 8 7 6 5 4 3 2 1

ISBN (hardback) 978-1-4222-4259-9
ISBN (series) 978-1-4222-4253-7
ISBN (ebook) 978-1-4222-7545-0

Cataloging-in-Publication Data on file with the Library of Congress

NATIONAL
HIGHLIGHTS

Developed and produced by National Highlights Inc.
Editor: Susan Uttendorfsky
Interior and cover design: Torque Advertising + Design
Production: Michelle Luke

QR CODES AND LINKS TO THIRD-PARTY CONTENT

TABLE OF CONTENTS

KEY ICONS TO LOOK FOR

Words to Understand: These words with their easy-to-understand definitions will increase the reader's understanding of the text while building vocabulary skills.

Sidebars: This boxed material within the main text allows readers to build knowledge, gain insights, explore possibilities, and broaden their perspectives by weaving together additional information to provide realistic and holistic perspectives.

Educational Videos: Readers can view videos by scanning our QR codes, providing them with additional educational content to supplement the text. Examples include news coverage, moments in history, speeches, iconic sports moments, and much more!

Text-Dependent Questions: These questions send the reader back to the text for more careful attention to the evidence presented there.

Research Projects: Readers are pointed toward areas of further inquiry connected to each chapter. Suggestions are provided for projects that encourage deeper research and analysis.

Series Glossary of Key Terms: This back-of-the-book glossary contains terminology used throughout this series. Words found here increase the reader's ability to read and comprehend higher-level books and articles in this field.

AWARENESS OF THE CAUSE

In an advanced society such as the United States, it is the responsibility of the nation to provide the most vulnerable in society with the same opportunities as the more abled. People with disabilities have the right to a reasonable standard of living, education, health care, and the support they need to have a full life. Professionals who make a career in working with people with disabilities make it their responsibility to enhance the lives of those in their care regardless of wealth, religion, or race.

"My advice to other disabled people would be, concentrate on things your disability doesn't prevent you doing well, and don't regret the things it interferes with."
– Stephen Hawking

"Believe you can, and you're halfway there."
– Theodore Roosevelt

"A hero is an ordinary individual who finds the strength to persevere and endure in spite of overwhelming obstacles."
– Christopher Reeve

"Optimism is the faith that leads to achievement. Nothing can be done without hope and confidence."
– Helen Keller

CHAPTER 1

Is a Career Helping Those With Disabilities For You?

Most people have a worthy cause that they believe in. You can even work in this field yourself by following a career and making a difference to those in need.

- Start out as a volunteer.
- Seek out a personal connection in the field.
- Develop an inspirational mission statement for yourself.
- Find out about the education, training, and qualifications required for your chosen career.
- Study job specifications of interest.
- Discuss your goals with your loved ones.
- Approach school counselors, charities, and organizations to obtain advice.

DISABILITY STATISTICS

About 56.7 million people–19 percent of the population–have a disability, according to a broad definition of disability.

DISABILITY IN THE UNITED STATES

People in the oldest age group—80 and older—were about eight times more likely to have a disability as those in the youngest group—younger than 15 (71 percent compared with 8 percent). The probability of having a severe disability is only one in 20 for those 15 to 24 while it is one in four for those 65 to 69.

- **Adults age 21 to 64 with disabilities have median monthly earnings of $1,961 compared with $2,724 for those with no disability.**

- **Difficulty with at least one activity of daily living is cited by 9.4 million noninstitutionalized adults. These activities include getting around inside the home, bathing, dressing and eating. Of these people, 5 million need the assistance of others to perform such an activity.**

- **About 15.5 million adults have difficulties with one or more instrumental activities of daily living. These activities include doing housework, using the phone, and preparing meals.**

Source U.S. Census Bureau.

DISABILITY AGE GROUPS

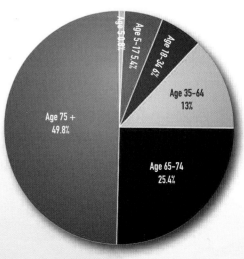

Age 5-17 5.4%

Age 5 10%

Age 18-34 6%

Age 35-64 13%

Age 75 + 49.8%

Age 65-74 25.4%

Source U.S. Census Bureau.

DISABILITIES

The Americans with Disabilities Act is a milestone law that guarantees equal opportunity for people with disabilities.

- About 8.1 million people have difficulty seeing, including 2 million who are blind or unable to see.

- About 7.6 million people experience difficulty hearing, including 1.1 million whose difficulty is severe. About 5.6 million use a hearing aid.

- Approximately 2.4 million have Alzheimer's disease, senility, or dementia.

- Being frequently depressed or anxious such that it interferes with ordinary activities is reported by 7 million adults.

- 41 percent of those age 21 to 64 with any disability are employed, compared with 79 percent of those with no disability.
  Source: U.S. Census Bureau.

TOP 10 CAUSES OF DISABILITY IN THE U.S.

1. Arthritis and rheumatism
2. Back or spine problems
3. Heart trouble
4. Lung or respiratory problems
5. Mental or emotional problems
6. Diabetes
7. Deafness or hearing problems
8. Stiffness or deformity of limbs or extremities
9. Blindness or vision problems
10. Stroke

Source: Spinalstenosis.org

DID YOU KNOW?

- People with disabilities are more likely to experience persistent poverty.

- People with disabilities often experience discrimination and prejudice.

- People with disabilities often find others stereotype them.

- People with disabilities often find the physical environment difficult to access.

AWARENESS OF THE CAUSE

6 Social Workers

1 Physical and Mental Health Services

5 Occupational Therapy

WHERE DO PEOPLE WHO ARE DISABLED GET SUPPORT?

2 Charities

4 Helplines

3 Support Organizations

WHAT DO PEOPLE WHO ARE DISABLED NEED TO REACH THEIR FULL POTENTIAL?

- Equality
- Individualized support
- Good health care
- Access to information
- Practical help

- Education opportunities
- Work opportunities
- Independent living support
- Good public services
- Financial support

THE BENEFITS OF HELPING OTHERS

A SENSE OF PURPOSE

Giving to others provides a sense of purpose to an individual. People who volunteer for a cause feel that their life is worthwhile and satisfying. This ultimately leads to improved physical and emotional health.

EMOTIONAL HEALTH

Studies have also shown that the act of charity results in emotional well-being. The person who gives to charity feels improved self-esteem. This gives a feeling of satisfaction to the individual. In a way, giving to others allows the individual to create a "kindness bank account." The more kind acts are filled in the account, the better the emotional state of the person.

A HEALTHY HEART

A recent study found that there is a significant correlation between helping others and the heart's health. It was found that people who volunteer are about 40 percent less likely to develop high blood pressure as compared to those who do not volunteer.

HELPING OTHERS MAKES YOU HAPPY

According to research, people who engage in acts of kindness and giving are happier in general as compared to others. Acts of kindness carried out regularly or even once a week can lead to greater happiness and joy in life.

REDUCE STRESS

The act of helping others can also help reduce stress. Research shows that people who help others have lower cortisol levels. The presence of this hormone in the body causes it to create feelings of anxiety and panic, which can lead to higher blood pressure levels. People who do less for others have a higher level of the stress hormone in their body.

Milestone Moment

SIGNING OF THE AMERICANS WITH DISABILITIES ACT (ADA), JULY 26, 1990

President George H. W. Bush signed the Americans with Disabilities Act into law on July 26, 1990. The ADA was the world's first law created to protect the rights of people with disabilities. Prior to the signing of this act, people with disabilities were often excluded from activities that other people were able to participate in, including basic rights like housing, education, employment, medical care, and other areas of life. Historically, families were encouraged to be ashamed of their disabled family members, and this attitude unfortunately crept its way into the actions of many people in power. The ADA made it illegal for people to be discriminated against due to a disability.

President George H. W. Bush signing the American with Disabilities Act (ADA).

WORDS TO UNDERSTAND

autism: a developmental disorder that affects a person's ability to interact and communicate with others

decibels: a unit of measurement of the volume of sound

manifest: to display or show in one's appearance

progressive: in medical terms, a disease or condition that is predicted to get worse or more severe over time

CHAPTER 2

Helping Those with Disabilities: Why It's Needed

PRIOR TREATMENT OF PEOPLE WITH DISABILITIES

When we take a look through history, it's easy to see that people with disabilities have not always been treated with fairness and respect. For many centuries, families were responsible for caring for family members with disabilities on their own, and in many societies, having a disabled family member was seen as a source of shame. In more modern years, government assistance was available to people with disabilities, but it was often abused. Landlords would accept the government money and then leave the disabled person to starve or freeze to death in an attic or other locked space.

A DAY IN THE LIFE: LAWYER FOR PEOPLE WITH DISABILITIES

When you imagine a lawyer in their day-to-day work, you probably think of them giving speeches in a courtroom. While this certainly can be a part of a lawyer's day, most of their time is actually spent writing, doing research, and meeting with clients, especially because lawyers usually work on many cases at one time.

Lawyers who work with people with disabilities may defend them against discrimination that has occurred in housing, employment, education, government, and social work situations. Lawyers can also work to change current laws. This type of work includes doing lots of research, meeting with people in power (such as politicians and policymakers), and giving speeches to groups of people who have the ability to change laws. Lawyers typically work long hours and find their work to be quite rewarding.

The abuse of people with disabilities was often overlooked by law enforcement officials.

Parents of children with disabilities were told by medical professionals that they lacked the money and resources to properly take care of their child. These doctors encouraged parents to have their child institutionalized, and sometimes family visited every once in a while. Little attention was paid to children with disabilities beyond their basic care—food, clothing, and a bed.

While things have changed greatly for people with disabilities, many still experience discrimination and hardship regularly in their lives. Society has made great shifts in how people with disabilities are treated, but there is still much work to be done. Today, there are many different careers that function to serve those who have disabilities. Some careers help people with disabilities to get government aid, to ensure that they are being treated fairly, or to help them learn how to modify their environment to suit their needs. Other careers work with people who have specific disabilities, such as Down syndrome or **autism**. There are also lawyers who help people with disabilities, fighting for them to get what they rightfully deserve after they are discriminated against.

If you're interested in working with people with disabilities, you're in the right place. As you read about different types of disabilities and the available career choices in this book, consider what topics stand out to you. It's important to consider whether you'd like to work with many different people with different types of disabilities, or if you are more interested in specializing in working with people who have just one specific type of disability.

MENTAL ILLNESSES

Mental illnesses such as generalized anxiety disorder, bipolar disorder, schizophrenia, obsessive compulsive disorder, and other mood/thought issues can be debilitating. People who suffer from these disabilities often suffer in

Society has made great shifts in how people with disabilities are treated. However, while this is positive, many people with disabilities still experience discrimination and have to fight for equality.

Total blindness is the total inability to see, or see light from dark. Visual impairment or low vision is a severe reduction in vision that cannot be corrected with standard glasses. Visually impaired people find it difficult to do certain tasks.

silence. Even the people close to them may not know what they're going through. This type of disability is different from others since it does not **manifest** itself physically. Disabilities that are not immediately apparent are known as "invisible," but that doesn't make them any less serious or difficult to live with.

Since there is still a stigma surrounding mental illness in the United States and Canada, some people who suffer do not seek treatment out of fear of what others will think. This can result in them not getting the help that they need to live a full and healthy life.

VISUAL IMPAIRMENTS

When we hear the term "blindness," we typically think of a person who is completely unable to see. While some people do have complete blindness and cannot see anything at all (including light), there are varying levels of vision impairment that qualify as a disability. People with partial blindness have limited vision but still need assistance. In the United States, people who have vision that is worse than 20/200 are considered legally blind. Certain people are born blind, but for others, the condition comes on gradually. Then there are those who go through a long period of vision loss before they become legally or completely blind. Accidents, glaucoma, diabetes, and injuries are all potential causes of blindness that can occur throughout a person's lifetime.

HEARING IMPAIRMENTS

Hearing impairments and deafness are similar, but deafness is more severe. People who experience hearing loss below 90 **decibels** are considered hearing impaired, while those who experience hearing loss above 90 decibels are considered deaf.

When someone is hearing impaired, their disability can be caused by problems in the ear, their nervous system, or a combination of the two. Hearing impairment is categorized as mild, moderate, or severe/ profound, depending on how well the person is able to hear the sounds that make up speech patterns.

People who have hearing impairments often need people to advocate for them in schools. Because children with hearing impairments typically speak later than other children, educators sometimes believe that their intelligence or ability to learn is compromised, but this usually is not the case. People who have a hearing impairment or deafness are usually just as intelligent as their peers.

Sign language is a means of communicating by people who are deaf or have hearing impairments. It uses gestures, facial expressions, and body language.

STUTTERING

Stuttering is a speech disorder that is classified by repetitive sounds, the absence of sound at unusual times during speech, and prolonged sounds at uncommon times during speech. Stuttering may not seem like a huge deal, but to those who suffer from this condition, it can be debilitating.

Many people who stutter struggle to interact with their teachers and peers, which creates social and learning difficulties that can affect them much longer than their school-age years. While scientists aren't completely sure what causes stuttering, they believe that there is a genetic link—60 percent of people who stutter have a family member who also stutters. While the disability is hard to reverse, it's far from impossible. Many people who stutter eventually overcome their condition with the help of a speech therapist.

Stuttering is a speech disorder that can be very debilitating and hard to cure. However, the condition can be successfully treated with the help of a speech therapist.

HEART CONDITIONS

There are a number of potentially invisible heart conditions that can affect a person's daily functioning to the point that they are considered to be a person living with a disability. While many heart conditions do not affect a person's daily functioning, coronary artery disease, congestive heart failure, and arteriosclerosis can all be debilitating.

People with coronary artery disease often suffer from severe chest pain and have medical restrictions on the types of activities they can do safely. Congestive heart failure can affect many organs in the body other than the heart and can cause extreme shortness of breath that limits a person's daily activities. Arteriosclerosis is a group of heart conditions that can eventually result in a heart attack if not looked after properly.

CEREBRAL PALSY (CP)

This disability is typically caused by a brain injury that occurs before a person is born, and it's considered a movement disorder that can also affect posture and muscle tone. Many people with CP need to use a wheelchair for mobility.

Signs of CP typically begin to show up during the preschool years, when a child's parents and/or pediatrician notice that the child is not moving in the same way as other children. Very stiff muscles, very relaxed muscles, exaggerated reflexes, shaking, difficulty eating, and problems with speech can all be signs of CP. Because it's caused by a brain injury, there's no such thing as a "typical" case of CP. Some people with CP have

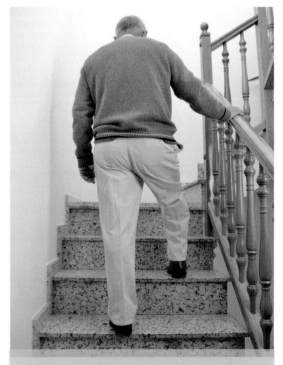

There are various heart conditions that can affect a person physically. Those afflicted often suffer from extreme shortness of breath and tiredness.

normal mental capacities, while others have learning disabilities. Some people with CP do not need any help in performing their activities of daily living, while others need live-in care.

CYSTIC FIBROSIS (CF)

Cystic fibrosis is a **progressive** disease that affects a person's lungs and their ability to breathe. CF is a genetic disorder, and while there is not currently a cure, researchers and doctors are working hard to create new medications and technologies to help extend the lives of people who have CF.

People who have CF often experience difficulty breathing, coughing, and frequent lung infections, such as pneumonia. Many times they also experience trouble gaining weight and difficulty properly digesting food. While many people with CF live to age forty or longer, there is no cure, and people with CF eventually die due to the disease.

MULTIPLE SCLEROSIS (MS)

MS is a nervous system disease. The central nervous system is made up of the brain, spine, and optic nerves. In most people, nerve fibers within the central nervous system are covered with myelin, a fatty substance that protects the nerves. In people with MS, inflammation damages the myelin, which can result in making it impossible—or nearly impossible—for the body to

Cerebral palsy is a disability caused by a brain injury before a person is born.

Cystic fibrosis is a genetic disorder that affects mostly the lungs, but also other organs in the body. The disease causes difficulty breathing and coughing, a result of frequent lung infections.

communicate with the brain. Some people with MS have mild symptoms and can generally live a normal day-to-day life, while other people with MS must use a wheelchair and may struggle to feed themselves.

Researchers aren't completely sure what causes MS, but it's likely that a combination of genetic and environmental factors are at work. There are many different treatments for MS, but researchers and doctors have yet to find a cure.

EPILEPSY

Epilepsy is a neurological disorder that causes seizures—a surge of electrical energy in the brain

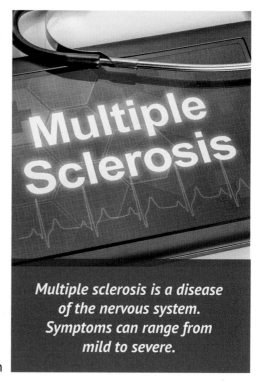

Multiple sclerosis is a disease of the nervous system. Symptoms can range from mild to severe.

that usually affects the way a person acts or appears for a period of time. Epilepsy is a chronic condition. People who have epilepsy experience seizures unpredictably and without any known cause. Sometimes people with epilepsy develop the disease after an injury, but often, the cause of a person's epilepsy is unknown.

Epilepsy is actually quite common—more than one out of every twenty-six people will develop the disease at some point over the course of their life. For about two-thirds of people who suffer from epilepsy, medication is effective in controlling seizures. Others may require surgery to control their seizures, while some are not helped by any known treatment. There is currently no cure for this disease.

MUSCULAR DYSTROPHY

Muscular dystrophy is a term meaning "progressive muscle weakness." Muscular dystrophy is actually a category of different diseases that affect the muscles. Most common in boys, muscular dystrophy may begin to cause problems in childhood. Sometimes it is not recognized until adulthood.

There is no cure for muscular dystrophy, but physical therapy, medication, and other treatments can help to slow the progression of the disease. There

Muscular dystrophy is a disease that affects the muscles, causing them to become weaker over time.

are differing levels of muscular dystrophy. Just like MS, some people who have muscular dystrophy can generally function well in their activities of daily living, while others may need to use a wheelchair and struggle to eat.

DOWN SYNDROME

Also known as Trisomy 21, Down syndrome causes a different path of development in an individual, both intellectually and physically. There are varying degrees of Down syndrome. Some individuals have a mild case, while others are more severe.

People with Down syndrome typically are smaller than other people, have eyes that slant upward, have less muscle tone than other people, and have a deep crease in the palms of their hands. Experts aren't sure exactly what causes Down syndrome, but they do know that the older the mother is, the higher the chance of a child being born with this disability.

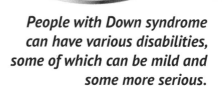

People with Down syndrome can have various disabilities, some of which can be mild and some more serious.

Most people with Down syndrome have some level of cognitive impairment. This may affect their speech and their memory. There is no cure for Down syndrome, and currently, the medical community thinks of Down syndrome as a condition, not a disease.

SPINA BIFIDA

Spina bifida is a birth defect that occurs when the spinal cord and the spine do not form properly before a baby is born. An organ called the "neural tube" normally closes in the first month of fetal development, but in a baby with spina bifida, the tube does not close at all. Some forms of spina bifida are extremely mild, and people do not find out they have it until they're getting an X-ray for an unrelated reason later in life.

Stroke victims often find themselves with some disability. This can include memory loss, paralysis, partial paralysis, and muscle weakness.

Other forms of spina bifida can be quite severe and can cause a baby's nerves and tissues to be exposed outside of their body at birth. This exposure can lead to life-threatening complications or death. Some cases of spina bifida fall in between these two extremes.

STROKE

A stroke is also known as a "brain attack." Strokes occur when blood flow is cut off from the brain. When the brain does not have access to oxygen, brain cells begin to die. The resulting damaged areas can cause problems with movement, muscle control, and memory, depending on which area of the brain is affected. While having a stroke is not a disability by itself, some people who have a stroke find that the aftereffects leave them with a disability. Paralysis, partial paralysis, and muscle weakness are all disabilities that can occur from a stroke.

PARAPLEGIA

A person who has paraplegia is partially paralyzed, meaning they are unable to move their body from the waist down. People who have paraplegia often need a wheelchair for mobility, or they may use crutches to walk. Many people who have paraplegia start off in a wheelchair but are able to build strength and find a new way to walk after physical therapy.

Paraplegia is usually the result of an injury or damage to the spine or brain. The majority of people who have paraplegia have healthy legs, but when the spinal cord is injured, it can be difficult for messages about movement to get to the brain. Paraplegia can also be caused by genetic disorders, autoimmune disorders, childbirth complications, and strokes.

QUADRIPLEGIA

People who have quadriplegia experience paralysis of their arms and legs. People who have quadriplegia are often paralyzed completely below the neck and are unable to move on their own. Quadriplegia is typically caused by an injury to the upper spinal cord. The higher an injury occurs on the spinal cord, the more damaging and/or life-threatening the injury will be. Spinal cord injuries that occur near the top of the spine often cause immediate death.

Just like paraplegia, people who have quadriplegia typically have healthy arms and legs, but damage to the spinal cord no longer allows their bodies to communicate properly with their brains. Many people who have quadriplegia

People with paraplegia are unable to move from the waist down.
This is usually the result of an injury.

struggle with depression, anxiety, chronic pain, and weight gain. It's key for people with this condition to join support groups to talk with others who understand what they are going through.

CHRONIC PAIN

For most people, pain alerts us to the fact that there is a problem in or injury to our bodies. For people with chronic pain, this isn't the case. Pain is classified as chronic when it lasts for longer than twelve weeks. There are a variety of different health conditions that can cause someone to experience chronic pain. Sometimes it stems from an injury, but other times, there is no known cause.

For some people, chronic pain is constant. For others, it can change from day to day depending on stress levels, humidity levels in the weather, and other things that may be going on in the body. People who struggle with chronic pain also tend to experience anxiety, depression, and fatigue and may struggle with professional and personal relationships.

People who suffer from chronic pain find it difficult to live a normal life. They often experience mental health problems and fatigue as a result.

NARCOLEPSY

Narcolepsy is a type of sleep disorder in which a person doesn't sleep the same way as a typical person. Their brains have trouble controlling their sleeping and waking cycles. This can result in a variety of symptoms, such as unwillingly falling asleep during daily activities, being very tired during the day even after a full night of rest, sudden muscle weakness while they are awake,

People who have narcolepsy struggle with their sleeping routine. They can unwillingly fall asleep, and when they do, they can experience vivid dreams.

and vivid dreams at night. People who have narcolepsy sometimes struggle to do certain kinds of jobs, especially those that involve driving.

Brain injuries and immune disorders can trigger narcolepsy, but scientists aren't completely sure what causes this disorder. There is not currently a cure, but there are many different treatments and lifestyle modifications that people with narcolepsy can use to control the disorder.

MIGRAINES

A migraine is more than just a headache—they cause pain that can

A migraine is a severe headache with a number of other symptoms including loss of vision and sensitivity to light and sound.

be debilitating. Sometimes migraines also cause loss of vision. When experiencing a migraine, many people also have extreme sensitivity to light and sound.

Migraines are likely caused by a combination of environmental, chemical, and genetic factors. Many people find it impossible to do their job or participate in activities of daily living while dealing with a migraine. For four to seventy-two hours, depending on the person and the severity of the migraine, a person can be incapacitated by pain from a migraine.

CHRONIC DIZZINESS

Also known as "vertigo," chronic dizziness is often caused by an inner ear issue, which may be present at birth or the result of an injury later in life. People who suffer from vertigo experience chronic feelings of nausea,

Suffering from chronic dizziness is often caused by a problem in the inner ear. It is a condition that can hinder a person's daily routine.

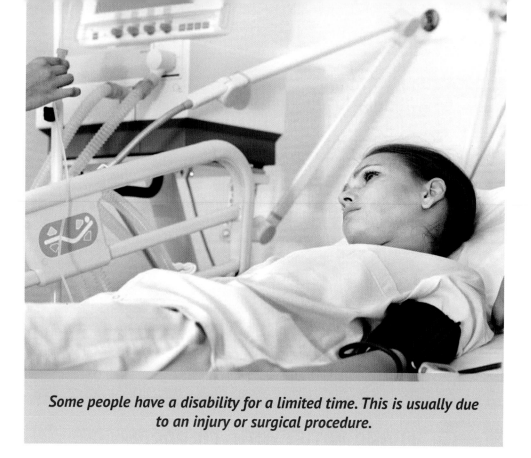

Some people have a disability for a limited time. This is usually due to an injury or surgical procedure.

dizziness, and the sensation that the world around them is tilting, spinning, or swaying. Vertigo can make it difficult for a person to go about their activities of daily living. This disability can be caused by many different health conditions, and sometimes it occurs seemingly for no reason at all. In time, vertigo usually goes away on its own.

IMPERMANENT DISABILITIES

While we often think of disabilities as permanent conditions, some disabilities last only for a certain period of time, and these are known as impermanent disabilities. Injuries that require a person to use crutches or a wheelchair for a time fall into this category. It's also possible for some disabilities to be healed—especially mental illnesses such as depression and anxiety.

WHAT IS THE CORRECT WAY TO REFER TO A PERSON WITH A DISABILITY?

Over the years, there has been a shift in how we refer to people who are disabled. In years past, it was commonplace to use the term "disabled person." Today, medical professionals and people who deal with disabilities prefer to use the term "person with a disability," as this puts their personhood first, not their disability. It's important to also use this format when referring to a specific disability. For example, it's correct to say "person with autism," rather than "autistic person."

LIVING WITH CYSTIC FIBROSIS

Watch this video to get a firsthand look at what it's like to be a teenager living with cystic fibrosis

TEXT-DEPENDENT QUESTIONS

1. What is the genetic cause of Down syndrome?

2. What is a symptom of muscular dystrophy?

3. What does it mean if a condition or disease is progressive?

RESEARCH PROJECT

Choose one of the disabilities in this chapter, and research different treatment approaches. How is treatment now for the condition different than it was fifty years ago? What are the latest advancements in research for this condition? Based on your research, do you think a cure is likely to be found in the next ten years? Why or why not?

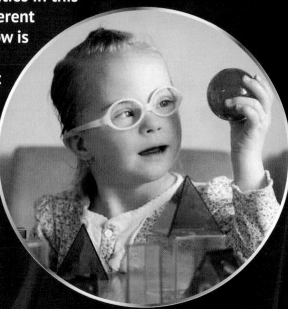

Milestone Moment

SIGNING OF THE INDIVIDUALS WITH DISABILITIES EDUCATION ACT (IDEA), 1975

IDEA is an important act that requires all public schools to provide an education to eligible children with disabilities.

Formerly known as the Education for All Handicapped Children Act, IDEA instilled a few important principles into place within the United States public education system. First, it required that all public schools make a free public education available to all eligible children with disabilities. Second, it required that this education be provided in the least restrictive environment possible.

Prior to this act, students with disabilities were often placed in special education classrooms even when it wasn't necessary. This meant that students with disabilities were not getting the same education as their typically abled peers. For instance, students with epilepsy may have been placed in a special education classroom even though their disability did not affect their ability to learn in the same way as their peers. The signing of IDEA was a huge step in the right direction for the United States government in ensuring that students with disabilities receive the education to which they are entitled.

intellectual disability: significant limitations in both intellectual functioning and adaptive behavior, which covers many everyday social and practical skills

literacy: the ability to read and write

supported living: a living environment for people with physical or mental disabilities; provides mental and physical health support

CHAPTER 3

Volunteering and Organizations

VOLUNTEERING

Are you nervous about volunteering to help people with disabilities? This is totally normal. While everyone feels apprehensive about any new experience, it can be especially nerve-racking when you're working with a brand-new group of people, since you aren't sure what to expect from people who are different than you. When someone looks, sounds, or acts differently from you or the people you typically interact with, you also may be unsure how to react, and that's ok. As you grow more comfortable working with people who are different from you, you'll see that you have many things in common. People who live with disabilities have the same emotions, hopes, dreams, and frustrations as people who do not have disabilities. You may be fearful that you'll react "incorrectly" to a person who is disabled, but even when you make mistakes, your being there is likely to make a positive impact in their life.

Before you begin to work as a volunteer, your volunteer supervisor will meet with you to tell you more about the work you'll be doing and train you on the tasks you'll accomplish during your shift. It's likely that you'll be a part of a group training with other people who are just getting started with their volunteer experience. It's great to take notes and ask questions while you're being trained so that you can learn as much as possible.

If you're feeling especially anxious about getting started, talk with your volunteer supervisor. They'll be able to offer you some suggestions specific to your situation to help you feel more comfortable. They may be able to match you up with a more experienced volunteer who you can work with until you feel comfortable working a shift on your own. Many people with disabilities would prefer that you ask them question about their condition rather than make assumption or try not to look at their physical disability. As long as you treat people with care and respect, it's unlikely that you'll offend anyone you're trying to help.

Before you begin to work as a volunteer with people who are disabled, you will have to do some training to equip yourself for the work at hand.

If you're in high school or college, volunteering is a great way to get some field experience before beginning your career. Many volunteer opportunities can count as high school or college credit. If you're interested in volunteering for class credit, talk to your academic adviser or guidance counselor about how the process works at your school.

Volunteering to help children who are disabled is a rewarding and worthwhile cause.

When working as a volunteer, it's important that you keep information about the people you work with private. Your volunteer supervisor will educate you on what information you can tell others about your work and what information needs to be kept confidential. If you're working in a residential or outpatient health-care facility, there are laws in place about what you can and cannot say to others regarding the health conditions of the people you work with.

ORGANIZATIONS

VOLUNTEERS OF AMERICA

Volunteers of America provides many services for people who are living with disabilities, including in-home care, day programs, employment, **supported living**, foster care, and case management. The organization's supported living facilities are homes for people who need long-term supported mental health care, such as people who are living with **intellectual**

A DAY IN THE LIFE:
SPECIAL EDUCATION TEACHER

A special education teacher typically arrives to work early, before students are ready to enter the classroom. They spend this time getting the classroom ready for students, writing the day's objectives on the board, and grading student work if they have any extra time. When it's time for the day to begin, students enter the classroom and the teacher begins working through the daily schedule. Sometimes there are unplanned breaks in the schedule that are necessary to help students with disabilities cope with behavioral and emotional issues. Often, special education students spend the majority of their day in the classroom with their teacher but go to other areas of the school for special subjects, such as art and music.

While the children are at other classes, a special education teacher works hard to accomplish a great number of tasks—grading student work, planning lessons, creating worksheets, cleaning the classroom, meeting with administrators, or calling parents to update them on a student's progress.

Special education teachers are also responsible for creating IEPs, or Individualized Education Plans, for their students. These documents dictate how all educators in the building need to work with the student to accommodate their disability.

disabilities. They also provide in-home care to people who need a lower level of support, such as help with home care, money management, or involvement in social activities.

Some people who volunteer with Volunteers of America are professionals who lend their services as a gift, such as therapists, nurses, and other mental health professionals. Other volunteers are students or people with careers in other fields who want to give back to their communities. Getting involved with Volunteers of America is an excellent way to get an idea of whether or not the field of working with people with disabilities might be a good career choice for you.

MEALS ON WHEELS

Meals on Wheels is a program in which volunteers deliver hot meals to people who are unable to easily leave their homes. There is more to the position than simply dropping off meals, however. Volunteers are encouraged to stay and talk with their clients, sometimes enjoying a meal with them, and sometimes helping them with things around the house, or even just sitting down to talk for a few minutes about how their day is going.

When a disability renders someone unable to leave their house, a Meals on Wheels volunteer may be the only face-to-face interaction they have throughout the day. This in-person touchpoint can be the difference between someone having something to look forward to and simply counting the hours until the end of the day. As a Meals on Wheels volunteer, you have the chance to be the bright spot in a person's day.

Meals on Wheels volunteers deliver hot meals to people who find mobility challenging. Volunteers use the time during the visits to have a conversation with their clients and check on their general well-being.

GIGI'S PLAYHOUSE

Gigi's Playhouse is a network of Down syndrome achievement centers. The "Playhouses" are run by volunteers, and there are many different opportunities to get involved. Each Playhouse has a schedule of programs during the week. Since the programs are run by volunteers, there are many opportunities to shadow experienced volunteers and learn the ropes. Volunteers set up, run, and take down programs every day.

Gigi's also offers **literacy** tutoring. If you love to read, you may be able to share your love of reading by teaching others. If you prefer office work, Gigi's also offers administrative volunteer opportunities. These volunteers run the office, answer the phone and emails, and process client paperwork. Want to volunteer with a club, youth group, or group of friends? Gigi's offers group volunteer opportunities that may be perfect for you. If you're interested in working with children with intellectual disabilities, Gigi's Playhouse is a good place to explore if a career in this field might be a good fit for you.

EASTERSEALS

Easterseals is an organization that advocates for and supports people living with disabilities. The organization is largely supported by volunteers. The Easterseals organization works to support people with disabilities in five different areas: where they live, work, and play and how they learn and act. In the "live" category, the Easterseals organization provides services to adults with disabilities—such as people with autism—and seniors by offering residential rehabilitation, physical health, and mental health resources.

Gigi's Playhouse uses volunteers to help people who have Down syndrome read.

In the work category, Easterseals provides people with disabilities with intellectually and developmentally appropriate workforce development opportunities, allowing people to grow and develop skills that will make them successful in the workplace.

In the play category, the organization offers camping opportunities for people living with disabilities, respite services for their caregivers, and emotional support, allowing people who have

Easterseals is an organization that provides opportunities and support for people with a range of disabilities.

similar abilities to come together and have a sense of community with one another.

In the learn category, Easterseals offers tools for families and parents who have family members with disabilities to get information on how to best support them. And in the act category, Easterseals takes legal action to ensure that people with disabilities are supported as legally required.

Easterseals offers a number of volunteer opportunities for people who are interested in working with those who have disabilities. Volunteer commitments are flexible—some volunteers work with the organization long term, while some volunteer do so when they have free time, without a long-term commitment. There are Easterseals organizations all over the country, and there is likely to be one with a variety of different volunteer opportunities in your area.

WHAT IF I'M NOT OLD ENOUGH TO VOLUNTEER?

Many volunteer organizations have age restrictions. If you're not old enough to volunteer but would still like to help organizations that help people with disabilities, fundraising is a great way to show support. Talk to your guidance counselor or teacher about holding a bake sale or other fundraiser to raise money for the charity of your choice.

LIVING WITH DOWN SYNDROME

Glimpse what life is like for people living with Down syndrome

TEXT-DEPENDENT QUESTIONS

1. Why is it important to keep patients' health information private when you're volunteering?

2. What services does Gigi's Playhouse provide for people with Down syndrome?

3. Easterseals advocates for people with disabilities. What does the word "advocate" mean?

RESEARCH PROJECT

Choose one of the organizations listed in this chapter, and research its history. How did the organization get started? How many years has it been in existence? How many chapters does it have across the United States and Canada?

SUPREME COURT CASE OF *TENNESSEE VS. LANE*, 2004

In 2004, the Supreme Court heard a case in which individuals sued the State of Tennessee. At that time, many state courthouses were not accessible to people with disabilities. In one case, a plaintiff was not able to access the courthouse due to their disability. The plaintiff refused to be carried up the courthouse steps to appear in court, which led to them being arrested.

The Supreme Court ruled that the state did indeed need to make its courthouses accessible to all. The ruling said that inaccessible courthouses were unconstitutional, as the 14th Amendment of the U.S. Constitution states that all United States citizens have the right to due process, and this means that they must be able to access a courthouse. This decision set a new precedent throughout the United States when it came to accessibility in government buildings.

Newly built government buildings must be made accessible for people with disabilities by law.

WORDS TO UNDERSTAND

accessible: easily able to be used

antecedent: a preceding event, condition, or cause

dissertation: a long essay written as a part of the completion of a doctorate degree

CHAPTER 4

Education, Training, and Qualifications

EDUCATION

HIGH SCHOOL GRADUATE

For high school graduates, there are many opportunities to work with people with disabilities. Many of the careers at this education level are direct-care opportunities, meaning that they involve working one-on-one with people with disabilities, assisting them in their activities of daily living. Many people who work in jobs at this level are in the process of furthering their education.

Working at the direct-care level is a great idea for someone who eventually would like a college-graduate– or advanced-degree–level job in the

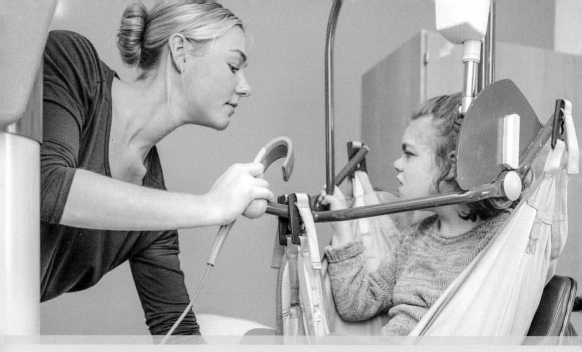

High school graduates who want to work with people with disabilities have a number of opportunities to choose from. Those who specialize in direct-care can expect to work on a one-on-one basis.

field. Direct-care provides the opportunity to get to know clients personally. This experience is indescribably valuable to people who eventually become in charge of other direct-care workers, such as doctors, researchers, mental health therapists, and directors of programs at charitable organizations.

Direct-care workers can work in a variety of settings, including inpatient or outpatient rehabilitation centers, nursing homes, or for home health care agencies. Some direct-care workers are also employed by hospitals as orderlies or nursing assistants. Direct-care workers are responsible for letting nurses, therapists, and doctors know about any new issues or needs a patient may have. Many direct-care workers develop close relationships with their patients.

In some schools, it's possible to work as a part of the learning support staff with a high school diploma. This is a great way to get started if you think that you might want to get certified to teach special education. Some schools will allow you to work as a classroom aide while you're in the process of getting your college degree. It may also be possible to work as a school nurse's aide at this level, depending on the requirements and restrictions of the school district in your area.

COLLEGE GRADUATE

Getting a college degree is important if you're interested in becoming a teacher to those with disabilities. There are different types of special education teachers.

Some teachers study general special education. In this type of program, the teacher-to-be learns about many different disabilities and about the different accommodations they will use to help students learn. Some special education teachers study a specific disability, such as hearing impairments or visual impairments. They become experts on how to help children with these specific disabilities learn at the same speed as their typically abled peers.

Becoming a special education teacher can be challenging. Since many special education classrooms are self-contained, these teachers must be able to teach all subjects well to students of varying academic and age levels. On top of this, special education teachers need to be able to handle behavioral and social issues that other teachers don't usually encounter. All of these facets are addressed in different college classes for special education teachers.

It's a good idea for teachers who do not anticipate specializing in special education to take some of these classes too. Many teachers will have students with mild to moderate disabilities in their classes at some point throughout their teaching career, even if they are not special education teachers.

In addition to special education teachers, some schools employ case managers. Case

For those wanting to be a special education teacher, a college degree is required. Special education teachers specialize in a variety of disabilities.

DAY IN THE LIFE: SOCIAL WORKER

For social workers, every day can look a little bit different than the last. At the start of the day, social workers typically look over their calendar and see when they have meetings planned with their clients. At these meetings, social workers sit down and talk with their clients through any life issues they may be having, as well as evaluate their treatment plans and progress toward their goals. Social workers are constantly adjusting treatment plans to help their clients make progress.

In between client meetings, social workers may make phone calls to community service providers to see if they are accepting new clients. A large part of a social worker's job is connecting people to community services that they need, and this can be hard in communities where lots of people need services. Social workers also communicate with the family members of their clients to update them on the client's progress.

Like many jobs in social services, social workers are also responsible for filling out copious amounts of paperwork to help their clients get the services that they need. Social workers also respond to emergency and crisis situations for their clients, which can mean that work often gets pushed until the following day or until late in the evening. Many social workers end up working far more hours each week than they had planned to due to the unpredictable nature of helping people in need.

managers are education professionals who have their degrees in special education or social work. They work with small groups of students and their teachers, creating IEPs for each student on their caseload to help the student move forward toward academic, social, and behavioral success. Some agencies that work with people with disabilities allow case managers and therapists to work with a college degree, especially if they are working toward getting their advanced degree at the same time.

ADVANCED DEGREE

Most of the career paths for working with people with disabilities require an advanced degree. There are several types of advanced degrees, but the three most common in this career field are master's degrees, doctoral degrees, and medical degrees.

Master's degrees typically take two years to complete. Doctoral and medical degrees take longer, between six and eight years, to complete.

Many of the careers in the field of working with people with disabilities require master's degrees. Physical therapists, occupational therapists, prosthetists/orthotists, speech therapists, mental health therapists, and some teaching positions all require at least one master's degree. Some people in these career fields also continue their studies to obtain a doctoral degree. Getting a doctoral degree involves more intense study than a master's degree, as well as completing a **dissertation**. Most people with doctoral degrees teach at a college or university as a part of their full-time job. Becoming a medical doctor involves many years of medical school, as well as on-the-job training.

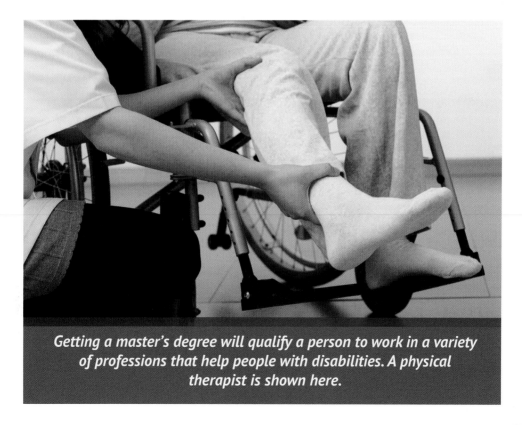

Getting a master's degree will qualify a person to work in a variety of professions that help people with disabilities. A physical therapist is shown here.

QUALIFICATIONS AND LICENSING

For most jobs working with people with disabilities, it's important to have a clean record and have your fingerprints registered with the state. Sadly, there have been many cases of people who have disabilities being abused by their caretakers. Having a clean criminal record and having fingerprints on file is one way that the government works to ensure that people with disabilities are being cared for by people who have their best interests at heart.

Many jobs at the college-graduate– and advanced-degree–level require licensing. Licensing requirements can be as simple as completing a course of study and filing an application with the state or as involved as taking and passing a series of complicated exams. Licensing requirements are often different from state to state. If you're interested in pursuing a career at the college or advanced level, be sure to research the licensing requirements in the state in which you'd like to work.

TRAINING

Depending on the career path you're interested in pursuing, there may be different trainings you're required to go through in addition to completing your educational program. The more you can dive into your training, the better. Training can be time consuming, but learning by

Most people who apply for jobs that involve working with vulnerable people will require a criminal record background check.

actually watching people on the job and practicing the job yourself will give you invaluable experience when the time comes to actually start your career.

STUDENT TEACHING

All teachers are required to complete a period of student teaching. This usually takes place over the course of a full academic year. In the first semester of the year, teachers in training watch a certified, licensed teacher. They observe different teaching methods, instruction styles, and ways to manage a classroom. Students in their first semester of student teaching often meet in small groups with other teachers in training, and together, they discuss what they're learning.

In the second semester of student teaching, teachers in training are often able to teach a few classes on their own—with a supervising teacher in the room. On a daily or weekly basis, the supervising teacher will talk with

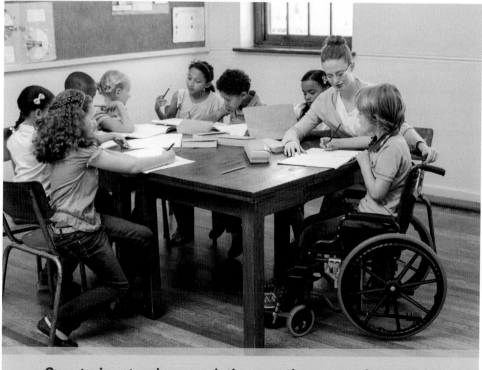

Once trainee teachers reach the second semester they are able to teach a few classes of their own with a supervising teacher in the room.

When students are on their practicum and internship, as part of the course, they meet in small groups to discuss their experiences.

the teacher in training about what went well and what needs to be improved. At the end of the student teaching experience, the supervising teacher will make a recommendation on whether the teacher in training is ready to handle a classroom on their own.

PRACTICUM/INTERNSHIP

In mental health careers and some health care careers, a practicum and internship experience is required. In practicum, the student watches an experienced person in the field. This may involve sitting in on mental health counseling or physical therapy sessions. They have the opportunity to ask the experienced person questions and may be able to help run some sessions themselves.

After successfully completing a practicum experience (usually over the course of a semester), they begin an internship where they actually perform the job under the supervision of an experienced professional. An internship can involve caring for patients, recording the ABCs of patient behavior (**antecedent**, behavior, and consequence), performing group therapy sessions, working with families, and doing home visits. The student needs to spend a certain number of hours working at practicum and internship. This number is determined by the academic program and the licensing requirements of the state.

During both their practicum and internship, students meet in small groups at their college or university to discuss their experience. They may also have to write papers or complete other assignments relating to their work. At the end of their practicum and internship experiences, the student is usually given a pass or fail grade by their supervisor.

RESIDENCY

In addition to internships, medical doctors also must complete at least a three-year residency. During residency, doctors work under the supervision of a more experienced doctor. Residency is usually done in a specialty area in which the doctor in training has chosen to focus. This time period can be a difficult part of a doctor's training, as they are still learning the ropes of the job and often balancing a large caseload of patients.

Medical doctors must complete a residency, and this is usually carried out in the medical field that they wish to specialize in. This doctor is a hearing specialist.

THERAPY FOR THERAPISTS

Many people are surprised to learn that going to therapy is highly recommended for mental health students by their professors. It can be hard to help others through their problems day in and day out, and talking through the stress that the job causes can be a key piece in avoiding burnout in the mental health career field.

HOW PEOPLE WHO ARE BLIND READ

People who are blind may use Braille to read. Learn more about what Braille is and how it works

TEXT-DEPENDENT QUESTIONS

1. What type of advanced degree requires a dissertation?

2. What is one career option at the high school diploma–level?

3. How long does it take to complete a medical degree program?

RESEARCH PROJECT

As mentioned in this chapter, abuse of disabled people is a sad reality that has happened on numerous occasions. Research what laws exist in your area to keep people living with disabilities safe from abuse.

Milestone Moment

FUNDING MADE AVAILABLE FOR WORLD WAR I VETERANS, 1918

Upon their return from World War I, many veterans found themselves dealing with a disability, no longer able to perform the job they had before they fought in the war. In order to help these veterans, the government began funding ex-military vocational training and job counseling. This helped veterans find and adjust to their new, postwar place in the United States.

In 1920, government funding for job counseling and vocational training was also made available to all people with disabilities. This was an important step toward equality for people with disabilities in the United States. The government recognized that people with disabilities could perform jobs just like a person without disabilities, and this change in attitude helped society as a whole begin to realize that people with disabilities may have different needs, but they are not inferior.

Following World War I, the government funded vocational training and job counseling for returning veterans.

WORDS TO UNDERSTAND

acute: symptoms that are severe but not long lasting

liaison: communication or a cooperative relationship between people who work closely together

government services: programs funded by local, state, or federal governments for people in need, including welfare, SNAP benefits (nutrition), and housing programs

CHAPTER 5

Salaries, Job Outlook, and Work Satisfaction

CAREER POSITIONS AVAILABLE

OCCUPATIONAL THERAPIST

Occupational therapists treat those who are dealing with injuries or disabilities by helping them through daily activities of living in a therapeutic way. Some occupational therapists work in hospitals, schools, and residential care centers, while others work in offices that do only occupational therapy.

Occupational therapists get to know their patients and develop plans for each one with goals that are challenging and achievable. For some patients, this may be learning how to walk after a traumatic injury. For other patients, this may mean learning how to speak after having a stroke.

DAY IN THE LIFE:
OCCUPATIONAL THERAPIST

An occupational therapist spends most of their day providing direct patient care. When meeting with a new patient, an occupational therapist will spend some time before the appointment going over the medical records to get a sense of the patient's needs and goals. While meeting with the patient, the therapist will evaluate their needs and talk with the patient about the goals that they are going to work toward with their treatment plan. These goals could be as complex as driving a car or as simple as brushing their teeth.

Occupational therapists also conduct home visits, evaluating a person's home environment so that they can make recommendations on how to change the home to better accommodate the person's needs. They may also evaluate the patient for special equipment needs, such as wheelchairs and walkers.

Occupational therapists report high levels of job satisfaction, even though their days are often long and require them to spend a lot of time on their feet. The average pay for an occupational therapist is $82,000 per year. This career field is growing rapidly, and it's likely that there will be 24 percent more job openings for occupational therapists in the next ten years than there are in the current job market.

PHYSICAL THERAPIST

Physical therapists help people who are injured or living with a disability to improve their movement skills and manage their pain. While physical therapists work with people with **acute** injuries, they also work with patients who are living with chronic conditions. They work closely with their patients' medical doctors, comparing notes and working together to come up with treatment plans. After talking with doctors, they'll design and implement a plan with their patient. These plans consist of exercises (usually stretching and strength training exercises) that the patient does in the office with the physical therapist, as well as exercises that the patient will do at home in between office visits.

At each office visit a patient has, the physical therapist has to evaluate how well the plan is working to ensure that they're making satisfactory progress. If the plan is not working well, the physical therapist needs to adjust the plan to meet the patient's needs. Since all patients are different, it usually takes some adjusting to figure out exactly what exercises the patient needs to make progress.

Physical therapists typically report a high level of satisfaction with their job, but some of them struggle with how physically demanding the job can be when they are providing direct patient care. The field of physical therapy is on the rise, and it's expected that there will be 28 percent more jobs for physical therapists in the coming ten years than there are right now. On average, physical therapists make $87,000 per year.

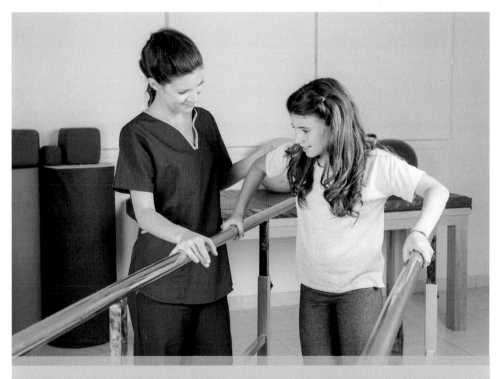

A physical therapist prepares a program for each patient in their care. Strengthening and stretching exercises aid rehabilitation.

SPEECH THERAPIST

Speech therapists, also known as "speech-language pathologists," are key members of the treatment team for many people who are living with disabilities. Speech therapists work to assess, diagnose, and treat speech and swallowing disorders in their patients. When speech therapists first begin to work with a new patient, they perform an assessment to evaluate the patient's speaking skills. They use this information to create a personalized treatment plan for that patient.

Just like a physical therapist, a speech therapist does some work in the office with their patients, but they also give their patients "homework" to practice skills in between office visits. At each office visit, speech therapists must evaluate how much progress their patient is making and adjust the treatment plan as necessary.

Speech therapists work in hospitals, schools, or other establishments where they are needed. They help people with speech and swallowing disorders.

Speech therapists can work in a variety of settings, including schools and hospitals. Speech therapists report a high level of job satisfaction. The field of speech therapy is growing, and it's expected that there will be 18 percent more speech therapist jobs in the coming ten years than there are currently. On average, speech therapists make $76,000 per year.

LAWYER

While the laws in the United States and Canada have come a long way in protecting people with disabilities in recent years, there is still work to be done. Lawyers can help people with disabilities in a number of different ways. Some lawyers, called "lobbyists," work to change laws so that they are better suited to help and protect people who are living with disabilities. They do research and meet with lawmakers to help them better understand the changes that need to be made to make life easier for those living with a disability.

Lawyers who specialize in representing people with disabilities work to protect the rights of their clients. Some lawyers work to change existing laws so that they are better suited to protect people with disabilities.

Other lawyers represent people with disabilities in court. If a person with a disability has been discriminated against, it's important that they have an experienced lawyer who understands their needs and is dedicated to fighting for their rights. While lawyers do spend some time in courtrooms, much of their time is spent researching laws and studying cases similar to the one(s) on which they are working.

Lawyers report differing levels of job satisfaction. One of the things that many lawyers struggle with is putting in long hours to the point where their personal lives are put on the back burner. Law careers are growing at an average rate—in ten years, there are likely to be about 8 percent more job openings than there are right now. On average, lawyers make $119,000 per year. It's important to note that lawyers who are just starting out and have not yet secured jobs at law offices typically make a much lower salary than this.

RESIDENTIAL CARE WORKER

Some people with disabilities are not able to live on their own, and so it often makes the most sense for these people to live in a residential care center. Residential care centers are homes for people who need the care of doctors and nurses, or other health-care professionals, around the clock.

These centers have many different job openings available, from event planners to those providing direct-care to administrative staff that communicates with the families of residents.

Residential care workers do all that they can to make the facility as home-like as possible. These workers plan special holiday celebrations, game nights, and administer medical care to their residents. Residential care workers report medium to high job satisfaction. Some workers in these facilities struggle with long hours and burnout.

Residential care careers are growing a bit faster than average. In ten years, it's predicted that there will be 11 percent more residential care jobs than there are right now. On average, residential care workers make $28,000 per year.

A residential care worker helps to provide a home-like environment for the residents that may include trips outside the center.

The role of a home health aide is to assist people who are disabled with their daily routine in their own homes.

HOME HEALTH AIDE

Many people with disabilities need some help with daily care, but not to the point where they need to live in a residential care center. Home health aides are health-care workers who visit people's homes on a daily basis to check on their needs and provide them with daily care. The responsibilities of a home health aide can be as simple to helping someone bathe or as complex as administering medication. Home health aides have a deep sense of care for their patients and often go above and beyond the call of duty to make sure their patients are well cared for.

Some home health aides help people with a variety of health conditions, while others work exclusively with one population, such as people with diabetes or the elderly. Home health aides report medium to high job satisfaction. Just like residential care workers, home health aides are susceptible to burnout. As more and more families choose to care for family members with disabilities in their homes, the need for home health care is growing quickly. In the next ten years, it's expected that the need for home health care workers will grow by as much as 41 percent. Home health aides are sometimes paid on a yearly basis, with an average salary of $23,000 per year, and they are sometimes paid on an hourly basis, with an average hourly wage of $11 per hour.

NURSE

Nurses who work with people with disabilities can be employed in a variety of settings, including nursing homes, schools, and home health care facilities. In addition to providing direct patient care, nurses serve as a **liaison** between the patient and their doctor, updating the doctor on the patient's needs and progress. Nurses also work to educate patients and their family members on how to care for their disability while providing emotional support.

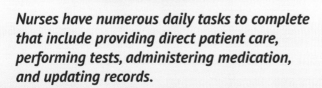

Nurses also administer medication, provide basic medical care, record patients' symptoms on their medical records, create care plans for patients, perform diagnostic testing and record results, and help patients understand and follow through with

Nurses have numerous daily tasks to complete that include providing direct patient care, performing tests, administering medication, and updating records.

aftercare plans for later when they are discharged from an inpatient health care facility. Nurses report medium to high levels of satisfaction with their jobs. Like many careers in the health-care field, nurses sometimes work very long hours and function on little sleep. This can cause burnout quickly. In the next ten years, it's expected that there will be 15 percent more nursing positions than there are right now. On average, nurses make a salary of $70,000 per year.

A career nursing people with disabilities is very rewarding. You will be providing medical care as well as emotional support.

Learning assistants who work with students with disabilities have a varied job specification. They can work on a one-on-one basis or help with a whole class.

LEARNING ASSISTANT

Learning assistants for students with disabilities may work in special education classrooms, or they may work with one student throughout the day. Some learning assistants work full-time, while others work part-time, assisting their assigned student only during certain classes. Learning assistants sometimes work with small groups of students who need extra help in learning a concept. Some learning assistants may help a number of different teachers throughout the day, rotating from classroom to classroom, or helping to supervise students during lunch, at recess, and on field trips. Learning assistants may also help students with disabilities with basic needs, such as eating and using the bathroom.

Job satisfaction for learning assistants is medium to high. It can be stressful to work with students with disabilities when they have behavioral issues, but it can also be incredibly rewarding to watch students make progress over time. The job outlook for learning assistants is average, and it's expected that there will be 8 percent more positions open for learning assistants in the next ten years than there are currently. On average, learning assistants make $26,000 per year when working full-time.

SOCIAL AND HUMAN SERVICE ASSISTANT

A social and human service assistant helps people who qualify for **government services** find and receive the aid that they need and are eligible for. Many people with disabilities qualify for a variety of government programs that can help them receive an income, education, and medical care. The paperwork that is required to receive these benefits can be quite daunting, especially for someone who has never navigated the world of government benefits before.

A social and human service assistant may work with a person's doctors, social worker, and/or mental health care provider to get the information they need to help a person receive benefits. They may also consult with a person's treatment team in order to provide input on treatment plans and find out how they can best help their

A social and human service assistant helps people with disabilities to receive the government aid that they are entitled to.

clients perform their activities of daily living. These assistants may help their clients get to and from medical appointments, go grocery shopping, and find and attend educational programs. They also check in with their clients regularly to ensure that they are receiving the services they have been promised.

Job satisfaction in this area is average—some social and human service assistants get frustrated at times because the pay they receive does not seem fair for the amount of work and dedication that they put into their job, but there is a great sense of satisfaction that comes from helping people in need. On average, social and human service assistants earn $33,000 per year, or $16 per hour. In the next ten years, social and human service assistant positions are expected to grow by 16 percent.

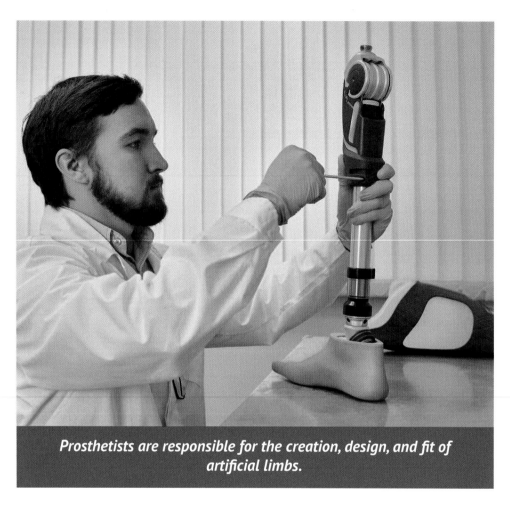

Prosthetists are responsible for the creation, design, and fit of artificial limbs.

ORTHOTISTS AND PROSTHETISTS

Orthotists design, create, and fit braces and other appliances to strengthen, support, or straighten patients' limbs. Prosthetists design, create, and fit artificial limbs for people who are missing limbs. Many of these professionals are currently working with people who have quadriplegia and paraplegia. While it sounds like something out of a science fiction movie, technology is being developed that will allow people who are paralyzed to move robotic limbs with their minds, allowing them to eat and perform other activities of daily living.

Orthotists and prosthetists can work in a variety of settings, including home health care stores, research laboratories, and hospitals. This field is growing much faster than average, and it's expected that in ten years, there will be a 22 percent increase in available positions for orthotists and prosthetists. Job satisfaction in this field is high. Many orthotists and prosthetists mention that they feel an extreme sense of pride when they see one of their clients walk again after being confined to a wheelchair for a long period of time. The average salary for orthotists and prosthetists is $66,000 per year.

REHABILITATION COUNSELOR

Rehabilitation counselors work with people with disabilities to help them live as independently as possible. Some rehabilitation counselors work with groups of people who all live with the same disability, while others work with people who have a variety of different disabilities.

Rehabilitation counselors may run therapy groups for people who have similar disabilities, facilitating

Rehabilitation counselors run therapy groups but also arrange one-on-one appointments with their clients.

conversation between group members to help them learn from one another's struggles and successes. During one-on-one appointments, rehabilitation counselors talk with patients and assess their needs, then create a treatment plan that may include accessing different services available to them in their communities. Just like any treatment plan provider, rehabilitation counselors must regularly follow up with their clients and adjust their plan to make sure it's continuing to meet their needs and help them progress toward independence.

Job satisfaction for rehabilitation counselors is high, and the job outlook is good—it's expected that in ten years, there will be 13 percent more job openings for rehabilitation counselors than there are right now. On average, rehabilitation counselors make $33,000 per year.

MEDICAL DOCTOR

Doctors who specialize in the treatment of people with disabilities may work in hospitals, research centers, or in private practice. Where a doctor chooses to work will determine what goes on in a typical day. For doctors who work in hospitals, much of their day is typically spent in providing direct patient care. This means that they are meeting with patients (and sometimes their families), evaluating their condition, and prescribing medical treatment. Doctors who work in hospitals are also an important part of treatment teams.

For patients who have complex medical issues, their doctor, specialists, mental health care providers, and community advocates often come together to develop an effective treatment plan. Treatment team meetings can take up a large portion of a doctor's day. In a hospital, an experienced doctor is also likely to be responsible for supervising interns and residents, as well as evaluating their performance and counseling them on how to best deliver patient care.

Doctors who work in research centers may also spend a large portion of their day meeting with patients, but they too meet with scientists and researchers to discuss potential new treatment options for patient care. They may also participate in clinical trials, in which they provide patients with new medication or treatment that is not yet available to the general public.

Doctors who work in private practice often have more of a say in how they

Medical doctors can choose to specialize in the treatment of people who are disabled. A doctor is a vital member of the treatment team.

spend their day, since they are usually the owner or co-owner of the practice. Doctors report medium to high job satisfaction. Some doctors work very long hours and struggle with burnout. The job outlook for doctors is higher than average, and it's expected that in ten years, there will be a 13 percent increase in job openings. On average, doctors make $208,000 per year.

SPECIAL EDUCATION TEACHERS

Special education teachers work in schools and teach children with disabilities. Some special education teachers work in self-contained classrooms, with a smaller number of students than regular education classrooms, where they teach students with a variety of disabilities in one room. This can be challenging, as these students often have different academic levels and are of different ages. Often, special education teachers also have one or two teachers' aides who help them in the classroom.

Special education teachers have a demanding role. They teach core subjects, such as reading, writing, and math to students with disabilities.

Clinical social workers provide people with disabilities much-needed assistance. They assess the needs of their clients and then design plans to meet those needs.

Some special education teachers do not teach all subjects to their students. They may teach core subjects, such as reading, writing, and math, and then students go to other classrooms for secondary subjects such as music, art, and social skills.

While special education teachers report having a deep sense of caring for their students, they often struggle with burnout due to a lack of support from the administration members at the school. In the next ten years, it's expected that there will be an 8 percent increase in the number of jobs available to special education teachers. On average, special education teachers make $59,000 per year.

CLINICAL SOCIAL WORKER

A clinical social worker's job sounds simple: they find people in the community who are in need of help, and they help them! When working with clients with disabilities, a clinical social worker's job can be wide-ranging. They meet with their clients regularly to assess their needs, and they design plans to meet those needs—getting their clients involved in receiving community services, finding or running therapy groups for their clients, and educating family members about how they can help their loved one with a disability. Social workers are also responsible for responding to emergency and crisis situations for their clients.

Over time, social workers follow up with their clients to ensure that their treatment plans are still effective and allowing them to make progress toward their goals. Social workers often feel a great sense of pride in the work that they do, but like many helping professions, they are often subject to burnout due to being constantly on call for their clients. The job outlook for social workers is good—it's expected that in the next ten years, there will be a 16 percent increase in the need for people in this career. On average, social workers make $48,000 per year.

When you see how much joy and happiness you bring to the people in your care, that's the most rewarding thing about working with people who are disabled.

SOME PEOPLE WITH DISABILITIES DO NOT HAVE FAMILY. WHO HELPS THEM?

It can be hard for anyone to make it through life without family support, but it is especially difficult for people with disabilities. Luckily, social workers, doctors, occupational therapists, and social/family services assistants all work together to ensure people with disabilities get the help that they need. When a person with a disability does not have a solid support system in place, their primary care doctor will often contact their practice's social worker to begin to establish a team to support the person.

LIVING WITH DISABILITIES

Living in a wheelchair can be challenging, but it doesn't stop people with disabilities from living their lives

TEXT-DEPENDENT QUESTIONS

1. Which of the careers listed in this chapter has the greatest potential for growth in the next ten years?

2. What does an occupational therapist do?

3. What's one task that a social worker may do in a typical day at work?

RESEARCH PROJECT

Choose one of the careers in this chapter, and interview someone in that field. Ask them to describe a typical day at work, things they like about their job, and things they wish they could change about their job. Based on your research, explain whether you think that job could be a good fit for you.

SERIES GLOSSARY OF KEY TERMS

abuse:	Wrong or unfair treatment or use.
academic:	Of or relating to schools and education.
advancement:	Progression to a higher stage of development.
anxiety:	Fear or nervousness about what might happen.
apprentice:	A person who learns a job or skill by working for a fixed period of time for someone who is very good at that job or skill.
culture:	A way of thinking, behaving, or working that exists in a place or organization (such as a business.)
donation:	The making of an especially charitable gift.
empathy:	The ability to understand and share the feelings of others.
endangered species:	A specific type of plant or animal that is likely to become extinct in the near future.
ethics:	The study of morality, or right and wrong.
food security:	Having reliable access to a steady source of nutritious food.
intern:	A student or recent graduate in a special field of study (as medicine or teaching) who works for a period of time to gain practical experience.
mediation:	Intervention between conflicting parties to promote reconciliation, settlement, or compromise.
nonprofit:	A charitable organization that uses its money to help others, rather than to make financial gain, aka "profit."
ombudsman:	A person who advocates for the needs and wants of an individual in a facility anonymously so that the individual receiving care can voice complaints without fear of consequences.
pediatrician:	A doctor who specializes in the care of babies and children.
perpetrator:	A person who commits a harmful or illegal act.
poverty:	The state of one who lacks a usual or socially acceptable amount of money or material possessions.
retaliate:	To do something bad to someone who has hurt you or treated you badly; to get revenge against someone.
salary:	The amount of money you receive each year for the work you perform.
sanctuary:	A place of refuge and protection.
stress:	Something that causes strong feelings of worry or anxiety.
substance abuse:	Excessive use of a drug (such as alcohol, narcotics, or cocaine); use of a drug without medical justification.
syndrome:	A group of signs and symptoms that occur together and characterize a particular abnormality or condition.
therapist:	A person trained in methods of treatment and rehabilitation other than the use of drugs or surgery.

ORGANIZATIONS TO CONTACT

National Federation of the Blind: 200 East Wells St. at Jernigan Place, Baltimore, MD 21230 Phone: (410) 659-9314 E-mail: pmaurer@nfb.org
Website: https://nfb.org

The American Chronic Pain Association: P.O. Box 850, Rocklin CA 95677 Phone: (800) 533-3231 E-mail: acpa@theacpa.org
Website: www.theacpa.org

Spina Bifida Association: 1600 Wilson Blvd., Suite 800, Arlington VA 22209 Phone: (800) 621-3141 E-mail: sbaa@sbaa.org
Website: http://spinabifidaassociation.org

Cystic Fibrosis Foundation (National Headquarters): 4550 Montgomery Ave., Suite 1100 N, Bethesda MD 20814 Phone: (800) FIGHT-CF E-mail: info@cff.org
Website: www.cff.org

National Down Syndrome Society: 8 E 41st St, 8th Floor, New York NY 10017 Phone: (800) 221-4602 E-mail: info@ndss.org
Website: www.ndss.org

Easterseals National Office: 141 W Jackson Blvd, 1400A, Chicago IL 60604 Phone: (312) 726-6200 E-mail: info@easterseals.com
Website: www.easterseals.com

INTERNET RESOURCES

www.ldworldwide.org
The official website for Learning Disabilities Worldwide provides resources, research, and support for those affected by learning disabilities.

www.ucp.org
United Cerebral Palsy's website provides resources and information on current public policy decisions that affect people living with cerebral palsy.

http://www.who.int/topics/disabilities/en
The World Health Organization provides information and statistics on how disabilities affect people worldwide.

www.specialolympics.org
The Special Olympics website provides interesting information on how sport can help create a world of inclusion, where all people are accepted, regardless of their ability or disability.

www.campvictory.org
A camp created for kids with special needs, Camp Victory's website provides information for potential volunteers and campers.

FURTHER READING

Carroll, Cathryn, and Susan Mather. *Movers & Shakers: Deaf People Who Changed the World*. San Diego, CA: Dawn Sign, 1997.

Keller, Helen, editor Candace Ward. *The Story of My Life*. New York: Dover Publications, 2018.

Hinson, Ted. *Beyond the Blindness: My Story of Losing Sight and Living Life*. Seattle, WA: Amazon Digital Services, 2017.

Lutkenhoff, Marlene, and Sonya Oppenheimer. *Spinabilities: A Young Person's Guide to Spina Bifida*. Bethesda, MD: Woodbine House, 1997.

Palacio, R. J. *Wonder*. New York City: Knopf Books, 2012.

INDEX

AUTHOR'S BIOGRAPHY

AMANDA TURNER lives in Dayton, Ohio, with her husband, son, dog, and cat. A former middle school teacher, she now enjoys traveling the country with her family wherever the Air Force chooses to send them! Amanda earned her BA in psychology from Penn State University and her MEd in school and mental health counseling from the University of Pennsylvania.

CREDITS